Study Guide for

IN GOD'S TIME

Study Guide for

IN GOD'S TIME

The Bible and the Future

Craig C. Hill

WILLIAM B. EERDMANS PUBLISHING COMPANY
GRAND RAPIDS, MICHIGAN / CAMBRIDGE, U.K.

© 2003 Wm. B. Eerdmans Publishing Co.
All rights reserved

Wm. B. Eerdmans Publishing Co.
2140 Oak Industrial Drive N.E., Grand Rapids, Michigan 49505 /
P.O. Box 163, Cambridge CB3 9PU U.K.

Printed in the United States of America

08 07 06 05 04 03   7 6 5 4 3 2 1

ISBN 978-0-8028-2654-1

www.eerdmans.com

Contents

Acknowledgments

Two of my colleagues at Wesley Theological Seminary, Bruce Epperly and Amy Oden, made several contributions to this study guide, for which I am grateful. I also wish to thank Jim Dake at Wesley for his encouragement and support. Last but not least, I would express my appreciation to Christine D. Pohl and Pamela J. Buck, whose study guide for the Eerdmans book *Making Room: Recovering Hospitality as a Christian Tradition* (Pohl, 1999) served as the primary model for this work.

Introduction

Authors often refer to their books as children. Publication is likened to birth or, better still, to that fateful day when a child leaves home to make her way in the world. We hope that we have prepared her well and that she will thrive, but the matter is not ours to control. Indeed, her future is largely unpredictable. She will go places that we have not anticipated, encounter persons whom we have never met, and do work that we could not imagine. Along the way, she will make friends with some people and, unfortunately, not with others. For parents, it is both an exciting and a daunting prospect. Of course, some degree of parental influence may continue even after adult children leave home. In terms of this analogy, this study guide is my attempt to provide long-distance parental support to my now independent offspring, to help the book to find its place and do its job.

That little bit of extra assistance is especially desirable since biblical eschatology, the subject of *In God's Time,* is unfamiliar to so many Christians. This fact was brought home to me last week when I visited a men's group that has been studying the book. The members, all of whom have been active churchgoers for decades, told me that the eschatological dimension of Christianity had come to them, quite literally, as a revelation. They had no idea previously of its centrality and importance to Christian faith.

I wrote *In God's Time* primarily for such persons. Eschatology is one of the most neglected and misunderstood topics within the mainline Christian denominations. The degree of neglect would be more understandable were the subject less significant. In fact, belief in God's final victory over evil, sin, and death is a core Christian affirmation. The degree of misunderstanding is easier to account for given the strangeness of apocalyptic texts such as Daniel and Revelation. Still, eschatology at its most basic level is not complicated, nor, for that matter, are the relevant biblical texts themselves impossible to comprehend.

Understanding the Bible — and Christianity with it — requires understanding eschatology. In one form or another, it is present in much of the second half of the Hebrew Bible and on nearly every page of the New Testament. It lies at the heart of contemporary debate concerning the "historical Jesus," and it plays a role in many of the theological controversies that define and divide Christians today. It is not the easiest subject in the Christian curriculum, but it repays its students in countless ways.

I hope that the following pages will stimulate and encourage readers in their study of this intriguing, multifaceted, and vital subject. I also hope that they will serve as both a useful overview and a helpful supplement to *In God's Time*. As the book's literary parent, I am grateful for this chance to introduce it to you.

Format

Two different models suggested themselves for this study guide. The first is the workbook, like the one provided to participants in the *DISCIPLE* Bible study series. The second is the teacher's guide, like those published in conjunction with school textbooks. Unfortunately, the cost of producing both a workbook and a teacher's guide is prohibitive. What has been created instead is a single volume containing key elements of both models. For example, the study guide's content and application questions can be used for individual reflection or group discussion — or both. The goal is to provide a flexible resource that will be helpful in a wide variety of situations.

Another decision concerned the division of the lessons. The simplest approach is to have eight lessons, corresponding to the book's seven chapters plus its conclusion and appendix. The difficulty with this approach is the fact that Chapters 3-5 contain a disproportionate amount of material that is likely to be new to readers. For that reason, I have sometimes recommended that groups split these chapters, yielding an eleven-lesson schedule. If twelve weeks are available, the book's conclusion and appendix ("Not Left Behind") also may be considered separately. In this study guide, I have again opted for a compromise. I did not split lessons 3-5, but I did expand them. Study materials related to the first and second halves of these chapters are distinguished from one another, making it easy for groups to divide lessons 3-5 should they choose to do so. Likewise, materials in the final lesson that deal with the book's conclusion are distinguished from those that deal with the appendix.

Each of the eight lessons contains the following elements:

- **Introduction**. A brief statement concerning the subject and purpose of the chapter.
- **Scripture Readings**. Three or four Bible passages related to the chapter. It is suggested that group meetings begin with one or more of these Scriptures, perhaps by reading one short passage in multiple versions.
- **Preview Questions**. My colleague Sharon Ringe often speaks of "beginning the journey at home," that is, starting our interpretation by considering what we already know and where we already stand. Each lesson includes a few questions meant to foster such reflection. Ideally, these should be considered prior to reading the associated chapter of *In God's Time*. For example, the last ten minutes of a group meeting could be used for discussion of one or more preview questions from the next lesson.
- **Main Points of the Chapter**. A summary of the chapter's major arguments and topics.
- **Content Questions**. Questions meant to encourage comprehension of the chapter.
- **Reflection and Application Questions**. Questions that get at the "So what?" issue. In what ways do the points raised by the chapter matter?
- **Activities**. Group exercises to stimulate and supplement discussion of the book. Such activities are particularly useful near the beginning of a meeting since they help group members to become acquainted and encourage them to participate in discussion.

The study guide closes with an appendix containing worship resources, including hymns and prayers related to the subject of eschatology.

Suggestions for Group Leaders

Most of what I can say about leading a study group is already known to anyone who has taught a church class or led a Bible study. ("Encourage everyone to participate in the discussion; ask open-ended questions; bring doughnuts," and so on.) Still, a few points are worth underscoring:

1. Over the years, I have visited several adult Sunday school classes in which a book was discussed that only a minority of the members had actually read. Needless to say, it was a less than satisfactory educational experience. Obviously, a certain level of individual commitment is required for group study to succeed. It may help to be explicit about your expectations in advance. Use of a "class covenant" — that is, an agreement in which members pledge to prepare faithfully for meetings — is widespread today. This model may not be appropriate to your situation, but its popularity highlights the need for consistent preparation by all group members.
2. The lessons that follow are merely suggestions. Moreover, they include many more questions than an average-length class is likely to cover. I encourage you to pick and choose, to abridge and expand as you see fit.
3. As I wrote in its preface, *In God's Time* is written from a "mainstream scholarly perspective." On the great majority of points, the book takes a moderate position, that is, moderate within the overall context of biblical scholarship. (I have received enough mail about the book to know that moderation is in the eye of the beholder!) That does not mean that I expect readers to agree with me at every point. Indeed, some, perhaps much, disagreement is inevitable (see *IGT,* p. 28). The challenge for group leaders is to create a safe atmosphere in which disagreements — with the book, of course, but especially amongst group members — are respected.
4. If all of the group members do not have this study guide, leaders might want to lift out one or two key questions from the upcom-

ing lesson that all participants can reflect on as they read the next chapter of the book. People often read more thoughtfully and carefully when they read for a specific purpose.

5. Finally, let me encourage leaders to vary the style of the sessions. A little creativity can go a long way toward making a lesson meaningful and memorable. To that end, I have included a few suggested learning activities for use with each lesson. Of course, not all of these exercises will work with every group. As always, it is up to the leader to discern what would prove most useful in his or her particular circumstances.

Sample Class Schedules

Below are two examples of the way that an adult-education class based on this study guide can be scheduled. For purposes of illustration, both classes begin at 9:00 a.m.

90-Minute Class:

Time:	Length:	Activity:
9:00	10 minutes	Welcome, Bible Reading, Prayer
9:10	20 minutes	Learning Activity or Small Group Discussion
9:30	15 minutes	Content Questions/Discussion
		What concepts do we need to understand?
9:45	30 minutes	Reflection and Application Questions
		What do we do with this information?
		Why does the chapter matter?
10:15	5 minutes	Conclusion — Sum Up Findings
		What did we learn?
		What do we need to do?
		What can we share with others?
10:20	10 minutes	Preview Next Lesson
10:30	—	End

60-Minute Class:

Time:	Length:	Activity:
9:00	10 minutes	Welcome, Bible Reading, Prayer
9:10	10 minutes	Learning Activity or Small Group Discussion

9:20	10 minutes	Content Questions/Discussion
		What concepts do we need to understand?
9:30	20 minutes	Reflection and Application Questions
		What do we do with this information?
		Why does the chapter matter?
9:50	5 minutes	Conclusion — Sum Up Findings
		What did we learn?
		What do we need to do?
		What can we share with others?
9:55	5 minutes	Preview Next Lesson
10:00	—	End

LESSON 1

Are We There Yet?

This short chapter focuses on the meaning and importance of eschatology (that is, belief in God's final victory over evil, futility, and death). It challenges both an "uncritical embrace" of eschatology ~ *God wins* on the part of some Christians and an "overhasty divorce" from it on the part of others. It also highlights problems with traditional eschatologies that modern believers must face squarely as they think about this vital subject.

Scripture Readings

Isaiah 60:18-22 *in His time*
Mark 1:14-15 *time has come*
1 Corinthians 15:1-20

Preview Questions

1. In what ways have you already encountered the subject of the "Last Days"? What did you carry away from that encounter?
2. How have your experiences encouraged or prevented you from believing that God is present and active in this world? Do you find it compelling to say that, in the end, "God wins"?

7

3. What words and images come to mind when you think about the subject of "The Bible and the Future"?
4. As you look toward the next decade, what are your images of the future? Are they hopeful? Hopeless? Ambivalent?
5. What are your grounds for hope?

Main Points of the Chapter

1. Interest in the End Times is at perhaps an all-time high.
2. Despite the record-breaking sales of Last Days books and merchandise, many Christians find the subject off-putting, confusing, or offensive.
3. Eschatology, the belief that "God wins," is at the heart of traditional Christian proclamation.
4. The event that most shaped the early Church's eschatology was the resurrection of Jesus.
5. The problems with traditional eschatologies (e.g., their view of time, cosmology, and creation) need to be confronted forthrightly by contemporary Christians.

Content Questions

1. What is the present state of thinking in the church on the subject of the future?
2. What is "eschatology"?
3. Explain and evaluate the statement, "Christianity is irreducibly eschatological."
4. What is the significance of Jesus' resurrection in Christian thinking?
5. What are some of the challenges facing traditional eschatologies?

Reflection and Application Questions

1. Why are End Times books so phenomenally successful? What do you see as their good and bad points?

2. Why do so many people either ignore or reject the Bible's teaching about the future? On what issues, if any, do you agree with their judgments?

3. Do you think that God has a plan for history? For your life? If so, do you have access to that plan? How?

4. What beliefs about the future are essential to Christianity? What beliefs are not?

5. What evidence is there that your beliefs are correct? What would it take to change your mind?

6. What do you hope to learn from *In God's Time*? What difference might it make to your faith, your understanding of the Bible, and your daily life?

Activities

1. Put a large sheet of paper on the wall or on a table and invite members, as they enter the room, to write answers (preferably using a marker) to an opening question such as "The future is . . . ," "I wish I knew . . . ," or "The Bible's teaching about the future is. . . ." Discuss the answers at the beginning of class.

2. Invite group members to talk about a resource that has shaped their thinking on this subject (e.g., a book or a film). Ideally, invite them to bring these resources to the first class for a period of "show and tell."

3. Show a short segment from an End Times film like *Left Behind* or *Thief in the Night*. What is the film's purpose? What feelings and conclusions does it elicit in viewers? How? Discuss how the film does or does not correspond to a proper understanding of biblical eschatology.

First Things First: The Bible

E very interpretation of the Bible, including the one attempted in *In God's Time,* is grounded in a prior understanding of Scripture. For example, what we make of a particular passage in Revelation has everything to do with what we already believe the book of Revelation to be. Putting first things first, then, means considering the nature of the Bible before undertaking a study of biblical eschatology.

Scripture Readings

Psalm 119:1-24
John 2:13-22 (quoting Ps. 69:9)
2 Timothy 3:14-17

Preview Questions

1. How was the Bible viewed and used in your childhood home? What other factors shaped your early impressions of the Bible?
2. Can you remember your first Bible? How and where did you get it?
3. Is Scripture an authority in your life? How do you understand the phrase, "the authority of the Bible"?
4. On a scale of 1 to 10, with "1" describing the viewpoint, "the Bible is entirely a human account of religious experience," and "10" de-

scribing the viewpoint, "the Bible is the inerrant Word of God," where would you place your own understanding of Scripture?

5. What are your impressions of those who do not share your view of Scripture? Do you regard such persons as believers? What are the boundaries of acceptable belief? How do you decide?

Main Points of the Chapter

1. Many Christians believe that the Bible contains no errors, discrepancies, or contradictions. This belief leads them to assume that the biblical authors share a single eschatology, which modern interpreters can piece together as they would a puzzle.

2. *In God's Time* does not presuppose that all biblical authors shared the same eschatology. Differing perspectives, where they appear in Scripture, should be respected and not artificially harmonized.

3. Inerrancy is a popular and imposing theory, but it does a surprisingly poor job of accounting for the Bible that we actually possess. A host of biblical "difficulties" can be explained if one does not assume that the biblical authors must agree on every point.

4. "Inerrantists" tend to think about the Bible deductively. Individual texts are interpreted in light of the already-accepted theory about the Bible. An alternative is to think inductively, weighing the evidence of individual texts before formulating a general view of the Bible.

5. A similar distinction can be made between those who would "conform" themselves to the Bible and those who would "model" themselves after it. While "conforming" may seem an attractive option, it greatly oversimplifies the process of biblical interpretation. "Modeling" is truer to the diverse biblical witness, although it does not yield the apparent certainty of results that is the strength of the "conforming" model.

6. Belief in the Bible is not an all-or-nothing-at-all proposition. Careful and responsible interpretation of the Bible does, however, require knowledge and effort.

Content Questions

1. What is Christian fundamentalism? The doctrine of biblical inerrancy?
2. Does biblical authority require biblical inerrancy? How do Christians differ in their understanding of authority?
3. What does the issue of inerrancy have to do with eschatology?
4. The book gives two examples of biblical "discrepancies" that can be explained historically. Do you know any other examples? What other "problem texts" can you list? Is it necessary to your faith to be able to formulate specific explanations for such difficulties?
5. What are the strengths and weaknesses of deductive and inductive approaches to the Bible? The strengths and weaknesses of biblical conforming and modeling?
6. How should we interpret the much-cited verse 2 Timothy 3:16?

Reflection and Application Questions

1. A Sunday school teacher has told your child that the Bible is either completely true or completely useless. How do you respond?
2. What images of the Bible do you find most helpful? Is the Bible a toolbox? A lamp? A pair of spectacles? A map?
3. Your pastor wants to lead a study on ethics using a best-selling book. Some church leaders say that Christian education should focus only on the Bible. Do you agree? Would it make a difference if the author of the book is or is not a Christian?
4. Do you believe that God still "speaks" to humans today? On what basis would you evaluate someone's claim to be speaking for God?
5. The incidence of divorce is high today, even amongst "Bible believing" Christians. Are Christians permitted to disagree with Scripture (e.g., Matt. 5:31-32)?
6. What are some of today's "but in Christ" questions? Why these?
7. If someone visited your church's worship service, what might he or she conclude about your view of the Bible? Why?

Activities

1. Divide the class into two halves and hold a pro-vs.-con debate on the subject of biblical inerrancy. (Divide the group arbitrarily; people should be assigned to a side whether or not they actually accept its position. In fact, it's a better exercise if they do not.) Each side should be given at least fifteen minutes to formulate its arguments, ideally in separate rooms. Both groups should then give a short opening statement, after which they may reply to the arguments of the other side. After several minutes, you might ask the two sides to switch positions. What important points did the other side omit from its argument?

2. Print out a few "problem texts" (e.g., the ones mentioned in the chapter) and discuss how persons representing different viewpoints might think about them.

3. Look at several ancient and modern statements of faith, including those published by individual churches. (Many churches now have websites that include their statement of faith. These can be found by doing an Internet search.) What do or don't the statements say about the Bible? Is the Bible an object of faith? Must members of the same church think alike about the Bible?

LESSON 3

The History of the Future

M any of the biblical writings deal in some way with the future. Naturally, this is true of the prophetic books, which are considered in the first half of this chapter. At least as important, however, are the covenant traditions of the Hebrew Bible, which gave Judaism a particular theological shape and a significant future orientation. The Babylonian Exile was thought to have been caused by the Jews' covenant infidelity, and the expectation of a renewed covenant and a restored Israel was foundational to subsequent eschatology, both Jewish and Christian.

As indicated in the Introduction, lessons 3-5 may be divided into two sections. For example, Chapter Three can be split into the following two lessons:

1. Prophecy, pp. 30-43
2. The Covenant Future, pp. 44-58.

Points that pertain to the second half of the chapter (i.e., "The Covenant Future," pp. 44-58) are marked below by an asterisk (*).

Scripture Readings

Donkey —

1 Samuel 9   *Genesis 15
1 Kings 18   *Exodus 19:1-8
Deuteronomy 18:15-22   *2 Samuel 7:1-17
                          *Jeremiah 31:10-34

14

Preview Questions

1. Where do you find people forecasting the future today? How do you evaluate their predictions?
2. What images does the word "prophet" bring to mind? What is "prophecy"?
3. Are there modern-day prophets? If so, can you give examples?
4. What is your view of history? Cyclical? Linear and heading toward its fulfillment? Absolutely determined, regardless of what we do? Meaningless?
5. Does God communicate with humanity today? Have you experienced God's guidance? If so, how?
*6. Have you ever felt that you were "in Exile"? Did it seem that you had been abandoned by God? If so, how did you regain a sense of God's presence?
*7. What covenants have you made in your life? What are characteristics of covenants?
*8. In your experience, is God's blessing dependent upon your obedience?
*9. Have passages in the Hebrew Bible about a coming age of restoration and renewal played a part in your own faith?

Main Points of the Chapter

1. It was common in the ancient world to believe that the future could be predicted. Many persons also believed that the future was determined by external forces (e.g., the Fates). Monotheistic religions vary in the way they understand freedom and/or predestination.
2. As a rule, the biblical prophets were more concerned about changing the present than predicting the future.
3. Prophecy existed in other ancient Near Eastern cultures and was similar in many ways to prophecy found in the Hebrew Bible.
4. It was not always evident which prophets were true and which were false, an issue that the biblical writers take up at numerous points and in various ways.
*5. The idea of covenant is basic to Judaism and Christianity. Many

covenants — including those to Abraham and Sarah, Moses and Israel, and David — have a future orientation.

*6. The "Mosaic covenant" linked (future) blessing to obedience. This is a central concept in Jewish and Christian thinking.

*7. The Davidic kingship ended with the Babylonian Exile. The expectation that an anointed one would arise who would re-establish the Davidic throne was basic to much messianic thinking.

*8. The destruction of the kingdoms of Israel and Judah raised the question of the permanence of the people's covenant with God. Prophets such as Jeremiah and Ezekiel foretold a renewal of the covenant in a gloriously restored Israel.

*9. Increasingly, the prophets imagined a renewed world in which God's righteousness would reign over all peoples. In this and other ways, they thought theologically about the future.

*10. In the work of the later prophets of the Hebrew Bible, we witness the beginnings of apocalyptic thought. A future is imagined that could be brought about only by an extraordinary act of God.

Content Questions

1. What is a prophet? What actions were typical of prophets?

2. In what ways was ancient Israelite prophecy similar to the kinds of prophecy found in surrounding nations? In what ways was it different?

3. What is fate? Fatalism? Predestination? Why do some monotheists believe in predestination? Why do others disagree? What is at stake?

4. What is the "Deuteronomistic perspective"? Where is it found? What are its strengths and weaknesses?

5. How did people attempt to distinguish between true and false prophecy?

*6. What is a covenant? What are the main features of the covenant with Abraham and Sarah? Moses and Israel? David? What do these covenants have to do with eschatology? What do they say about God?

*7. What is a "Messiah"? What does belief in a coming Messiah have to do with King David? Jesus?

*8. Why and in what ways was the Exile important for the development of biblical eschatology?

*9. What is "supersessionism"? Is Christianity inherently supersessionistic? How ought contemporary Christians to think about Judaism?

*10. How did prophecy change in the period during and after the Exile? How do you account for these changes? Why are they important to Christianity?

Reflection and Application Questions

1. Does God reward obedience and punish wrongdoing in this world?

2. How are we to think about uniqueness in religion? Is only what is unique true?

3. Does God communicate with us today? If so, how (e.g., dreams, visions, prophecies, coincidences)? How can we judge such claims?

4. Does God know the future? If so, is the future predetermined by God?

5. Who in your community (congregation, town, denomination) speaks the truth when it's a hard word? Is such a person a prophet?

*6. What are we to make of the fact that so many of the grand prophecies of Israel's restoration were not literally fulfilled?

*7. Is the covenant between God and Israel still in force? If so, in what way? Was God responsible for the establishment of the modern state of Israel? Do the Palestinians have a right to live in lands promised to Abraham in the book of Genesis?

*8. The kings of Israel and Judah were often opposed by prophets. Is there a conflict in your community/church/denomination between institutional and "charismatic" authorities? Are both types of authority necessary? Is one or the other usually right? How are such differences resolved?

*9. How are the prophets of the Hebrew Bible relevant to church and society today? Are some parts of their message more relevant than others?

*10. What is the relationship between theology and expectation for the future? Is such expectation necessary to Judaism and Christianity? Can such expectation change?

Activities

1. Brainstorm for several minutes about the "speed bumps" presented by the chapter (that is, the ideas and statements that caused readers to slow down and think — whether to agree, to clarify, or to object). Do not try to respond to the points immediately; instead, list them on paper or a blackboard and then see how many of them are addressed by the subsequent discussion. The group can return to the list near the end to see what still needs to be discussed. (Can be used with either half of the chapter.)

2. On p. 33, it is stated that prophets often said, in effect, "Here is what things will look like if you do not straighten up." Break into groups, asking each to compose one or more such "words" to the nation today. Consider points such as the following:

   • What sins must be addressed?
   • What are their inevitable consequences?
   • What would constitute repentance?
   • What would happen if the people were to listen to your message?

   Regather to discuss the work of the small groups.

*3. Distribute copies of a wedding service and analyze it as a covenant ceremony. What does it have in common with the biblical covenants? Is marriage itself a good analogy for our covenant with God?

LESSON 4

Apocalypse Then

Apocalyptic authors wrote about God's soon-coming intervention that will bring history-as-usual to an end and usher in a new era of peace, justice, and prosperity. Apocalyptic thought is evident in some exilic and post-exilic prophets (that is, those who were active during and after the Babylonian Exile) and was further developed in the three or four centuries before Christ. Knowledge of this movement is essential to understanding both the ministry of Jesus and the rise of Christianity.

Chapter Four can be divided into two sections, yielding shorter and more manageable lessons:

1. Introduction to Apocalyptic Thinking, pp. 59-74
2. 1 Enoch and Other Inter-testamental Jewish Literature, pp. 74-93.

Points that pertain to the second half of the chapter (i.e., "1 Enoch and Other Inter-testamental Jewish Literature, pp. 74-93) are marked by an asterisk (*).

Readers are encouraged to study at least a portion of the pseudepigraphical book 1 Enoch. An edition of R. H. Charles's translation is in print, and the full text is also available on the Internet. See the "Links" section of the www.InGodsTime.com website for details.

Scripture Readings

Ezekiel 36:16-38
Daniel 7:9-14
Malachi 4
Mark 13:14-27

Preview Questions

1. Does God have everything "under control"? What events would seem to confirm or disconfirm your conclusion? How do Christians account for evil? Is there a difference between human evils, such as murder, and "natural" evils, such as the death of a child from leukemia?
2. What images come to mind when you hear the word "apocalypse"?
3. Do you believe in life after death? If so, why and in what form?
4. Do you believe in the existence of evil powers (e.g., Satan and demons)? If so, what is their origin? Their fate?
*5. Do you have any prior exposure to ancient Jewish or Christian books that were not included in the Bible?
*6. What would you expect to find in such books? What wouldn't you expect?
*7. What do you think the Jews of Jesus' day expected to happen in the future?

Main Points of the Chapter

1. Apocalyptic thinking flourishes in times of turmoil and dislocation. Such thinking was widespread in the Judaism of the intertestamental period.
2. Although apocalypses varied considerably, it is possible to identify a number of elements that were common to them generally (see the list on pp. 61-63).
3. Apocalyptic texts wrestle with the problem of evil. They assert that "despite all appearances to the contrary, God has everything under control" (p. 63) and exhort believers to endure persecution.

4. Prophetic and apocalyptic texts may be distinguished from one another in certain ways, for example, in terms of "means and ends," which are more other-worldly in apocalyptic literature.

5. A number of the ideas and images common to Jewish and Christian apocalyptic writing were also found in surrounding cultures.

*6. 1 Enoch contains the earliest and most important of the non biblical apocalypses. The book was not composed at one time but instead contains Enoch traditions which originated over a period of two or three centuries.

*7. The figure of Enoch is similar to the "primordial sage" in other ancient Near Eastern cultures.

*8. The Similitudes (or "Parables") contains a portrayal of the Son of Man that is remarkably similar to that found in the New Testament. The Son of Man is also referred to as Messiah and Son of God.

*9. Many other parallels exist between the New Testament and 1 Enoch. The book is cited explicitly by the author of the New Testament book of Jude (vv. 14-15; see also v. 6).

*10. Seven key predictions common to apocalyptic literature are listed with examples taken from a range of ancient non-biblical works (pp. 87-92). Each of these points has counterparts in the New Testament.

Content Questions

1. What is "apocalyptic" literature? What are the core elements of apocalyptic writings? What is the difference between prophetic and apocalyptic literature?

2. When and how did apocalyptic thinking develop? In what ways was it subject to outside influences? What do you make of such influence?

3. What is "theodicy" and how is it related to eschatology?

4. What did apocalyptic writers have to say about the fate of outsiders, especially non-Jews? How do you evaluate their conclusions?

5. When did the idea of eternal life enter into Jewish thinking? What idea(s) did it replace? How did it vary amongst the apocalyptic writers?

*6. Who was Enoch? What is 1 Enoch?

*7. What is the origin and significance of the "Son of Man"?

*8. Who are the "Watchers"? Why do they figure so prominently in some apocalyptic writings?

*9. Why are many apocalyptic writers interested in the order of the universe (e.g., the movement of the stars)?

*10. What expectations were common to the apocalyptic writers?

Reflection and Application Questions

1. What vision of God is reflected in apocalyptic literature? How do you respond to that vision?

2. The book states that "Apocalyptic thinking flourishes in times of dislocation and crisis" (p. 63). Is that true today?

3. Do you believe in a future judgment of humanity? If so, who will be judged? On what basis? To what final destiny?

4. *When* are we living? For example, in the closing days of the old age? In the new age? In the still-early days of human history?

5. Which of the twelve characteristics of apocalyptic thinking (pp. 61-63) make sense to you? Which do not? Why?

6. Imagine being transported to the "heavenly realm." What questions would you ask? How are these similar to or different from those of the apocalyptic writers?

*7. What is the significance of texts like 1 Enoch for Christians? For example, do they explain or complicate, undermine or support Christian faith?

*8. Are all eschatologies apocalyptic? What would a non-apocalyptic eschatology look like?

*9. What surprised you when reading about 1 Enoch and the other non-biblical apocalyptic writings? What are the implications of these surprises for your understanding of Judaism and Christianity?

*10. Imagine that your pastor read a portion of 1 Enoch during a worship service. How would you respond? Do "non-canonical" books (that is, books not included in the Bible) such as 1 Enoch have a place in the church today?

*11. Which of the predictions listed on pp. 87-92 do you accept? Why these?

Activities

1. Distribute recent newspapers and news magazines. Which stories might be cited in support of apocalyptic thinking? Which stories might seem to discredit an apocalyptic perspective?

2. Ask class members to conduct an Internet search for some of the keywords from this chapter (e.g., "apocalypse," "apocalyptic," "judgment," "Watchers," etc.). (Different words can be assigned or members can be asked to pick out one or two words on their own.) Print out a few of the most interesting webpages and bring them to show to the group.

*3. Ask the group to compare the list on pp. 87-92 with the so-called "little apocalypse" of Mark 13. What are the similarities? Differences?

*4. *Is it in the Bible?* Mix quotations from non-canonical and biblical texts. Can group members tell which is which? On what basis? Are some of the non-canonical texts more similar to the Bible than others?

All in the Family: Daniel and Revelation

Having looked at other ancient apocalyptic writings, we turn to a study of the biblical apocalypses, Daniel and Revelation. The authorship of Daniel is an especially important and controversial subject. *In God's Time* takes the view shared by most non-fundamentalist scholars, namely, that Daniel was written in or about the year 165 B.C. by an anonymous Judean scribe. The book is a call to faith and obedience in the face of persecution, specifically, the attempt on the part of the Syrian king Antiochus IV to outlaw the practice of Judaism. The author of Revelation confronted a similar situation two centuries later, "re-dreaming" Daniel's dream in the context of Roman oppression. It follows that both books are best viewed as sources of theological insight, not historical foresight.

For those wishing to split this chapter into two lessons, the division is clear:

1. Daniel, pp. 94-110
2. Revelation, pp. 110-129.

Points that pertain to the second half of the chapter (i.e., Revelation, pp. 110-129) are marked by an asterisk (*).

Scripture Readings

Daniel 7:19-28
Daniel 12
*Revelation 13:1-10
*Revelation 21:1-5

Preview Questions

1. Are many sermons preached in your church on the books of Daniel and Revelation? Why?
2. What obstacles need to be overcome to understand Daniel and Revelation?
3. What stories come to mind when you think of Daniel? Why are the stories in the first half of the book so popular?
4. Based on your study of Chapter Four of *IGT*, what expectations do you bring to your study of Daniel?
*5. What do you think of when you hear the term "millennium"? "Armageddon"? "666"? "New Jerusalem"?
*6. What do you think is the purpose of the book of Revelation?
*7. Why do people disagree so sharply about the meaning of Revelation?
*8. Revelation was not included by some early Christians in their list of authoritative books (that is, their *canon*). What would Christianity lose were Revelation not in the New Testament? How would Christian history have been different?

Main Points of the Chapter

1. Daniel and Revelation tend to be regarded either as books of historical foresight or theological insight.
2. Genesis 1-3 presents a theology of human and cosmic origins. Likewise, apocalyptic texts such as Daniel and Revelation offer a theological account of human and cosmic destiny. In both cases, the authors made use of existing ideas to convey distinctive theological convictions.

3. The figure of Daniel appears in early Jewish literature prior to the setting of the biblical book of Daniel.

4. Apocalypses of the historical type are usually dated to that time when their predictions become inaccurate and stereotyped. Using this standard, most scholars date Daniel to about the year 165 B.C.

5. The narratives of Daniel 1–6 are different in many respects from the apocalyptic materials found in chapters 7–12.

6. The visions of Daniel center on the figure of Antiochus IV, who prohibited Jewish practice and desecrated the Jewish temple.

7. The author(s) of Daniel anticipated a soon-coming vindication of Israel and the resurrection of the most righteous and the most wicked.

*8. Revelation appears to have been written at the time of the Roman emperor Domitian. The situation in which Revelation was written is similar in many respects to that of the book of Daniel, composed more than two centuries earlier. The author of Revelation made extensive use of Daniel and other apocalyptically oriented biblical writings.

*9. Much of Revelation is taken up with descriptions of the judgments awaiting God's enemies, in particular, the emperor, the imperial cult, and the city of Rome.

*10. The church does not escape judgment entirely. The "letters to the seven churches" in chapters 2–3 contain both rebukes and exhortations directed at Christians.

*11. Revelation ends with a glorious vision of "the world reborn and Paradise revisited" (p. 127).

*12. Revelation does not provide us with a "road map" to the future; nevertheless, it is a valuable book that still challenges and inspires modern believers.

Content Questions

1. What does *In God's Time* mean by asking if Daniel and Revelation are books of "historical foresight or theological insight" (p. 95)? What do you think?

2. In what way(s) might the account of the future in Daniel and Revelation be likened to the account of creation in Genesis 1–3?

3. What is a pseudonymous writing? How does one judge authorship of such literature? How is a pseudonymous apocalypse dated?
4. When, where, and why was the book of Daniel written? How do the first and second halves of Daniel differ?
5. Who was Antiochus IV? What is his significance within the book of Daniel?
*6. When, where, and why was Revelation written? In what ways is Revelation similar to and different from Daniel?
*7. How have Christians managed to "domesticate" the book of Revelation?
*8. What are the "letters to the seven churches"? What is their value for Christians today?
*9. Who or what is the "beast"?
*10. Can Revelation be regarded as social and/or political commentary? What is Revelation's view of the Roman empire?
*11. What elements does Revelation share with earlier apocalyptic writings? In what ways is it distinctive?
*12. What is Revelation's vision of the future?

Reflection and Application Questions

1. What do you think of the ancient practice of pseudonymity? Is Daniel pseudonymous? If so, how does that conclusion affect your understanding and use of the book? Does the Bible contain other pseudonymous books?
2. What difference does it make to interpret Daniel in the context of ancient apocalyptic literature?
3. What do you make of the comparison between Genesis and apocalyptic writings found on the bottom of p. 96? If Genesis may be regarded as theology projected onto the past, is it appropriate to regard Daniel and Revelation as theology projected onto the future? Do such texts have to be historically accurate to be theologically true?
4. What view of the state is present in each of the two halves of Daniel? Which do you find more persuasive? How should Jewish and Christian believers today regard their governments? (See also Revelation 13.) How does your own social location affect your interpretation of books like Daniel and Revelation?

5. What hopes for the future are mentioned in Daniel 12? To what extent do your agree or disagree with this picture of the future?

*6. Is Revelation a pessimistic or an optimistic book?

*7. How compatible is the Jesus of Revelation with the Jesus of the Gospels?

*8. How do you respond to Raymond Brown's assertion that the author of Revelation "did not know how or when the world will end, and neither does anyone else" (p. 128)?

*9. It has been said that it is the job of preachers "to comfort the afflicted and afflict the comfortable" (p. 129). Whom does Revelation comfort? Afflict? In what areas might you and your church need comfort? Affliction?

*10. Is Revelation a dangerous text? Why or why not?

*11. What do you think the author(s) of Daniel would have to say to the author of Revelation? Where might they agree? Disagree?

*12. If Revelation were written today, who would be "the beast"? Why? What other contexts can you imagine that might yield different answers?

Activities

1. Imagine that you have been commissioned to create a short video on the subject of "Our Government." What images would you include? How might others choose to represent the government? Alternatively, draw a picture or construct a collage that characterizes your perspective on government. Another variation is to assign different persons or small groups a specific identity (e.g., a Muslim in America; a Christian in China, etc.).

*2. Break into groups. Each group is to write a letter to its own church(es) modeled on the seven letters in Revelation 2–3. What would be commended? Challenged?

*3. A number of Christian hymns are based on the book of Revelation. Distribute copies of a hymnal containing a Scripture index (e.g., *The United Methodist Hymnal*). Review the listings and consider how Revelation is used in Christian hymnody. Are certain passages or themes favored over others? Any surprises? If possible, sing one or two of the hymns as a group.

LESSON 6

Jesus and the Things to Come

A number of books published in recent years have re-popularized the idea that Jesus was essentially misunderstood by his followers and actually held no (or at most very few) eschatological beliefs. This theory flies in the face of the evidence and it is rightly dismissed. In fact, the thread of eschatology runs through both Jesus' teachings and his actions, and it links him believably to Judaism on one side and to Christianity on the other.

Scripture Readings

Mark 8:27-38
Luke 4:16-21
John 7:25-31

Preview Questions

1. Who is Jesus? What stories about Jesus are most meaningful to you?
2. What do you think Jesus knew about the future? Did Jesus have limitations?
3. What comes to mind when you hear the phrase "the kingdom of God"?

4. What is your image of judgment? Does judgment play a role in your spiritual life? Did Jesus believe in judgment?
5. What has Jesus already accomplished? What will he accomplish in the future?

Main Points of the Chapter

1. Two key questions in New Testament study are, "Was Jesus an eschatological figure?" and, "Did the early Christians, including the New Testament authors, get Jesus right?"
2. Christianity arose quickly and spread rapidly. These facts weigh against the notion that the early church fundamentally misunderstood and/or misrepresented Jesus.
3. Scholars have been unable to agree about the criteria by which to judge which sayings of Jesus are "authentic." As a consequence, there are nearly as many "historical Jesuses" as there are historical Jesus scholars.
4. A credible "historical Jesus" must fit within a certain historical space, being sufficiently the product of Judaism and adequately the cause of Christianity. The "eschatological Jesus" is such a figure, as many (probably most) scholars realize.
5. Jesus proclaimed the dominion of God, which was both present and future and which was characterized by reversal. Jesus' teaching also included mention of a future judgment.
6. Jesus believed that he himself would play a central role in the realization of God's reign — even despite his death, which he anticipated.

Content Questions

1. What is the significance of eschatology in the study of the historical Jesus?
2. What is "the dominion/kingdom" of God? How did Jesus characterize it?
3. In what ways was Jesus similar to John the Baptist? Different?
4. What evidence suggests that Jesus was an "eschatological figure"?

5. What is a "Son of Man"? What is a "Messiah"? Did Jesus think of himself as either?
6. What does it mean to say that "God's dominion is characterized by reversal"? Did such reversal include judgment?
7. When did Jesus expect the reign of God to come?

Reflection and Application Questions

1. What was the relationship between Judaism and Jesus? What are the dangers created by separating Jesus from his Jewish context?
2. What are the obstacles to creating the "historical Jesus"? How do you evaluate claims about the Jesus of history?
3. Did the early church fundamentally misunderstand and/or misrepresent Jesus? On what basis do you make that judgment?
4. Who did Jesus think he was and what did he think he was doing? In what sense, if any, do you believe that Jesus was and/or will be vindicated?
5. What is your response to Jesus' healing ministry? What did it have to do with the reign of God? Do such healings occur today? How do you understand the relationship between spirituality and health?
6. What response does Jesus' teaching on "eschatological reversal" demand from us?
7. What would it mean to take Jesus' teaching about the kingdom/dominion of God seriously? How would our priorities change? How would our churches be different?
8. What did Jesus expect to happen in the future? How do you evaluate that expectation? How does your evaluation correlate with your understanding of Jesus' divinity? Jesus' humanity?

Activities

1. Distribute blank cards or sheets of paper. Ask group members to write down five things that they are confident that Jesus did and five things they are confident that Jesus said. Collect the cards and read them aloud. How do they differ? Are any trends evident? What sorts of things are not mentioned? Why these?

2. Brainstorm about favorite Gospel sayings and stories. (Have someone list these on a blackboard or a large sheet of paper.) What picture of Jesus emerges? What kinds of sayings and stories were not
included? Was one Gospel favored over others? Why? How close is
our "favorite Jesus" to the "historical Jesus"?

3. Stage a short but somewhat complex event. (For example, three
people unfamiliar to the group could interrupt the meeting, ask
questions of different members, pick up one or two items, and
then leave the room.) Divide into groups and ask each group to
write a paragraph-long account of what just happened. Do the accounts differ? Why? Is it reasonable to compare these accounts to
the four Gospels? Why or why not?

LESSON 7

The Once and Future Kingdom

Like Jesus, the early Christians believed that the reign of God was both present and future. How they struck the balance between "realized" (what Christ has already accomplished) and "future" (what Christ has yet to accomplish) eschatologies was a significant factor in shaping their faith. The same is true of Christians today.

Scripture Readings

1 Corinthians 4:6-13
Romans 8:1-17
1 Timothy 1:8-14
Hebrews 1

Preview Questions

1. Are we already living in the New Age?
2. What is the significance of Jesus' crucifixion and resurrection?
3. How are Christians different from other people?
4. In what ways is God active in our world?
5. How does the Spirit equip Christians today?

Main Points of the Chapter

1. To a significant extent, the expectations of the early church mirrored those of Jesus himself.
2. The crucifixion and the resurrection of Jesus were regarded as eschatological work already done.
3. The early church's eschatology shifted over time, for example, toward a more realized eschatological perspective.
4. The distinction between future and realized eschatologies is evident in the New Testament as well as within contemporary Christianity. The tension between these perspectives may be regarded as a subset of the larger tension between material and spiritual accounts of reality.
5. The eschatology of the apostle Paul makes for an especially interesting study. Paul's emphasis on the cross led his thinking in the direction of a future eschatology. In other contexts, his emphasis on the present admission of Gentiles led his thinking in the opposite direction.
6. Two patterns of theological orientation correspond to future and realized eschatological perspectives. These are outlined on p. 190.

Content Questions

1. What is at stake in the claim that "Christianity is not discontinuous with Jesus any more than Jesus is discontinuous with Judaism" (p. 171)?
2. How did the early Christians interpret the crucifixion of Christ? What did the cross accomplish? The resurrection?
3. In what ways did the early Church's eschatological viewpoint(s) change over time? Why? How would you evaluate these changes?
4. What is the difference between a "realized" and a "future" eschatology? What are the strengths and weaknesses of each perspective? Which do you find more appealing? Convincing? Why?
5. In what ways is Paul an example of a Christian who has a foot "in both eschatological camps"?
6. What difference does it make in day-to-day life if we have a future or a realized eschatological perspective?

Reflection and Application Questions

1. Where do you locate yourself on the chart on p. 180? From your perspective, what is the right balance between the "already" (realized) and the "not yet" (future) eschatological perspectives? When do you "lean" on which "foot"?

2. For what should we pray? What is the relationship between divine action and the "natural" order of events? How does your worldview influence your understanding of eschatology?

3. What is the proper relationship between science and religion?

4. *In God's Time,* p. 194, states, "The relationship between Jesus and the early church is marked both by continuity and discontinuity. The same holds true of the relationship between ancient and modern Christians." Should we try to replicate the first-century church today? What does it mean to be faithful to the early Christians' example?

5. How do you evaluate Christian supersessionism (pp. 174-75)?

6. Where does your church fit on the chart on p. 190? Why? In your opinion, is your church located too much to one side of the chart?

7. Are Christians "only human" (see p. 192)? Are Christians acting naturally or unnaturally when they sin? Does the Spirit give believers power over (all) sin?

8. Are some sorts of prayers more likely to be answered than others? Why? How should we think about unanswered prayer?

Activities

1. Put up signs saying "Future Eschatology" and "Realized Eschatology" on opposite sides of the room. For each of the ten "Characteristic Elements" on p. 190 (e.g., emphasis on "Jesus' humanity" and "Jesus' divinity"), ask group members to stand at the point between the signs that they think corresponds to their own perspective. Discuss the results. Was there much movement from one "Element" to the next? Did the group largely stay together? On what point was there the most difference of opinion? The least?

2. Divide a blackboard into two columns headed "Questions answered by science" and "Questions answered by religion." Brain-

storm about what questions fit under each heading. Do any questions belong in both columns? Is science equipped to answer religious questions? The reverse? Why?

3. Discuss the following "case study": For seven years, the Reverend Smith has served as pastor at St. Philip's Church. It recently came to light that he left his previous church appointment in part because of an allegation of sexual harassment. The Reverend Smith has admitted that he made inappropriate advances a decade earlier toward a sixteen-year-old church member. "But I was forgiven by God and am now, by the power of the Holy Spirit, a changed man." As members of the church council, you have been asked to determine whether the Reverend Smith's pastoral appointment will be renewed.

Hope Unseen; Not Left Behind

A careful study of the biblical writings within their historical con-
text(s) does not yield a single eschatology. Indeed, the construc-
tion of a uniform "biblical eschatology" requires a distorting of the Bible's complex witness and a silencing of the Bible's distinctive voices.
Today's most popular eschatological system, called "premillennial
dispensationalism," does both. Hope in God's future does not require
us to systematize what is not systematic or to be certain about matters
that we may know only in part.

Points that pertain to the appendix, "Not Left Behind," are marked
with an asterisk (*) below.

Scripture Readings

Revelation 21:1-4
Revelation 22:1-7
*1 Thessalonians 4:13-5:11
*Mark 13:14-37

Preview Questions

1. What is faith? How is faith related to knowledge? To certainty?
2. Is the eschatological dimension of Christianity a burden or a blessing?

3. How are faith and hope related? For what do you hope?

*4. What have you heard or read about "the rapture"?

*5. Must certain events occur for Christ to return? If so, what are those events?

*6. What are the pluses and minuses of believing that Christ is about to return?

Main Points of the Chapters

1. Hope is not the same thing as certainty. There is much that we do not know about the future, but we may trust the future with God.

2. Hope in God's future does not excuse passivity. In fact, it demands a higher level of engagement in the present.

3. Jesus' demands were eschatological in character. Facing them requires eschatological resources.

4. Christianity is a religion of hope. To live Christianly is to experience newness of life *now*.

*5. Today's most popular form of eschatology, premillennial dispensationalism, goes back to the 1820s and 1830s.

*6. John Nelson Darby, founder of premillennial dispensationalism, believed that the expectations of Israel's restoration and glory found in the Hebrew Bible would be fulfilled literally after the dispensation to Israel recommenced.

*7. Darby argued that Christ would return twice, first in secret to "rapture" the church (thus completing the dispensation to the Gentiles) and then, a few years later, to reign on earth (thus completing the dispensation to Israel).

*8. Darby's approach is ingenious, but it flies in the face of the biblical witness. Like other harmonization schemes, it offers an interpretation that borrows widely from the biblical authors but which is actually foreign to all of them. The effort to create a single eschatological system silences the distinctive voices of the individual biblical writers. All too often, the presupposition of inerrancy compels biblical "literalists" to misread the Bible.

*9. It is only fair to acknowledge the benefits of premillennial dispensationalism, such as the urgency it lends to questions of Christian commitment and discipleship. On the other hand, it can produce negative effects, especially disengagement from the world's problems, which will soon be "left behind." We are fortunate that Darby's perspective was ignored by generations of Christian reformers.

Content Questions

1. What does it mean to say, "Hope that is seen is not hope" (Rom. 8:24b; p. 196)?
2. In what sense and for whom is eschatology a burden? A blessing?
3. The book states that "We are called to newness of life *now.*" In what ways is that statement true? False?
4. What is the relationship between Jesus' own eschatological perspective and the demands he places on disciples?
*5. What is "premillennial dispensationalism"? Where, when, and why did it develop?
*6. What is the "rapture"? What are some of the key passages cited in its defense? What questions does the book raise about the interpretation of these texts?
*7. What is "harmonizing" (p. 203)? Is dispensationalism "an elaborate harmonization strategy"? In what ways does the approach to the Bible taken in *In God's Time* differ from that found in dispensationalist books such as *The Late Great Planet Earth* and the *Left Behind* novels?
*8. What is the social and political agenda of popular dispensationalist authors? How does it show up in their work (e.g., the antichrist as General Secretary of the United Nations in the *Left Behind* novels of Tim LaHaye)?

Reflection and Application Questions

1. Does eschatological belief encourage social and political passivity? Why or why not?
2. Do you believe that "Eschatological demands require eschatological commitments and eschatological resources" (p. 198)? How do we get those resources?
3. What is the relationship between eschatology and ethics?

4. Evaluate the statement, "To live Christianly is to live hopefully" (p. 198).

*5. Why is premillennial dispensationalism so popular today?

*6. How ought we to think about "unfulfilled prophecy" (p. 201)? What are the strengths and weaknesses of Darby's approach?

*7. Is belief in the "rapture" a form of escapism? Why or why not?

*8. Reread the final paragraph (pp. 208-9). What "work" should we be found doing?

Activities

1. It is not unusual nowadays to see "rapture" bumper stickers, such as the popular "In case of rapture, this car will be unmanned." (Or the less common counter-sticker, "In case of rapture, may I have your car?") Try to sum up or characterize your own view of eschatology in a bumper-sticker saying. (I am no fan of sound-bite theologizing, but it is useful at times to clarify and organize our ideas by means of direct statements.) If possible, supply members with bumper-sticker sized paper and markers and ask them to share their results with the group.

2. The final class session should include time for summing up and looking ahead. What have we learned? How have our minds changed? What new questions do we now need to consider? What decisions face us? What do we need to tell others? What actions should we undertake individually and as a group?

*3. If you have not done so already, show a clip or two from "rapture films" like *Left Behind* and *Thief in the Night*. How do group members now evaluate such materials? How would you respond were one of these films to be shown to the junior high youth group at your church?

*4. Since the appendix is quite short, you might ask class members to read and discuss one or two supplemental articles, such as Tim Weber's important *Christianity Today* essay "How Evangelicals Became Israel's Best Friend." See the "Links to Related Sites" section at www.InGodsTime.com for hyperlinks to this and other relevant articles.

APPENDIX

Worship Resources

Prayers

O God, by whose command the order of time runs its course: Forgive, we pray thee, the impatience of our hearts; make perfect that which is lacking in our faith; and, while we tarry the fulfillment of thy promises, grant us to have a good hope because of thy word; through Jesus Christ our Lord.

Gregory of Nazianzen, 330-90[1]

Almighty God, give us grace, that we may cast away the works of darkness, and put upon us the armor of light, now in the time of this mortal life . . . that in the last day when he shall come again in his glorious majesty to judge both the quick and the dead, we may rise to the life immortal, through him who liveth and reigneth with thee and the holy ghost now and ever. Amen.

Thomas Cranmer, 1489-1556[2]

1. Frank Colquhoun, ed., *Prayers for Every Occasion* (New York: Moursehouse-Barlow, 1974), p. 26.
2. C. Frederick Barbee and Paul F. Zahl, *The Collects of Thomas Cranmer* (Grand Rapids: Eerdmans, 1999), p. 2.

Bring us, O Lord God, at our last awakening into the house and gate of heaven, to enter into that gate and dwell in that house, where there shall be no darkness nor dazzling, but one equal light; no noise nor silence, but one equal music; no fears nor hopes, but one equal possession; no ends nor beginnings, but one equal eternity; in the habitations of thy glory and dominion world without end.

John Donne, 1572-1631[3]

Glory to the Father, who has woven garments of glory for the resurrection; worship to the Son, who was clothed in them at his rising; thanksgiving to the Spirit, who keeps them for all the Saints; one nature in three, to him be praise.

Syrian Orthodox prayer[4]

O Lord, you have made us very small, and we bring our years to an end like a tale that is told; help us to remember that beyond our brief day is the eternity of your love.

Reinhold Niebuhr, 1892-1971[5]

Christ, thou hast bidden us pray for the coming of thy Father's kingdom, in which his righteous will shall be done on earth. We have treasured thy words, but we have forgotten their meaning, and thy great hope has grown dim in thy Church. We bless thee for the inspired souls of all ages who saw afar the shining city of God, and by faith left the profit of the present to follow their vision. . . . Show thy erring children at last the way from the City of Destruction to the City of Love, and fulfil the longings of the

---

3. George Appleton, ed., *The Oxford Book of Prayer* (Oxford: Oxford University Press, 1988), p. 165.

4. *Oxford Book of Prayer*, p. 255.

5. *Oxford Book of Prayer*, p. 164.

prophets of humanity. Our Master, once more we make thy faith our prayer: "Thy kingdom come! Thy will be done on earth!"

Walter Rauschenbush, 1861-1918[6]

O Thou who art the hope of the world, hasten, we beseech thee, the coming of thy kingdom upon earth. Establish thy rule within us; enter into our minds with thy truth, and dwell in our hearts with thy righteousness and compassion. Establish thy rule in our midst; enter into our homes, our schools and churches, our industry and commerce, all our cities and countries, that the world may be turned from the paths of destruction toward the shining city of God; through Jesus Christ our Lord. Amen.

Ernest Fremont Tittle, 1885-1949[7]

Thou hast promised to wipe away all tears from our eyes.
    I ask Thee to fulfill that promise now.
Thou hast promised to bind up our wounded spirits.
    I ask Thee to fulfill that promise now.
Thou hast promised to give us peace, not as the world gives
        but in the midst of our trouble.
    I ask Thee to fulfill that promise now.
Thou hast promised to be with us alway.
    I therefore thank Thee that Thou art walking beside me
        every step of the way.
I put my hand in Thine, and walk on into the future, knowing
that it will be a good future because Thou art in it. Amen.

Peter Marshall, 1902-49[8]

6. Walter Rauschenbush, *For God and the People: Prayers of the Social Awakening* (Boston: Pilgrim, 1910), pp. 107-8.

7. Ernest Fremont Tittle, *A Book of Pastoral Prayers* (Nashville: Abingdon, 1951), p. 84.

8. Catherine Marshall, ed., *The Prayers of Peter Marshall* (New York: McGraw-Hill, 1954), pp. 60-61.

Grant that we may neither be too much lost in regrets for the past nor dreams for the future, but grant that we may do with our might that which lies to our hand, so that we may fight the good fight, and finish the race, and keep the faith, and so at the end receive the crown of righteousness which you will award to those who have been faithful. This we ask for your love's sake. Amen.

William Barclay, 1907-78[9]

Almighty God the Father, through your only-begotten Son Jesus Christ you have overcome death and opened the gate of everlasting life to us. Grant that we, who celebrate with joy the day of our Lord's resurrection, may be raised from the death of sin by your life-giving Spirit; through Jesus Christ, our Lord, who lives and reigns with you and the Holy Spirit, one God, now and forever.

Lutheran Worship, 1982[10]

O God, who gave us birth,
you are ever more ready to hear than we are to pray.
You know our needs before we ask,
and our ignorance in asking.
Show us now your grace,
that as we face the mystery of death
we may see the light of eternity.

Speak to us once more your solemn message of life and of death.
Help us to live as those who are prepared to die.
And when our days here are ended,
enable us to die as those who go forth to live,
so that living or dying,

---

9. William Barclay, *Prayers for the Christian Year* (New York: Harper ChapelBooks, 1964), p. 15.

10. *Lutheran Worship* (St. Louis: Concordia, 1982), p. 49.

our life may be in Jesus Christ our risen Lord.
Amen.

Book of Common Worship, 1993[11]

Scripture Sentences

Psalm 42:5-6a
Why are you cast down, O my soul,
and why are you disquieted within me?
Hope in God; for I shall again praise him,
my help and my God.

Isaiah 60:18-19
Violence shall no more be heard in your land,
devastation or destruction within your borders;
you shall call your walls Salvation,
and your gates Praise.
The sun shall no longer be your light by day,
nor for brightness shall the moon give light to you by night;
but the LORD will be your everlasting light,
and your God will be your glory.

Isaiah 66:22-23
For as the new heavens and the new earth, which I will make,
shall remain before me, says the LORD;
so shall your descendants and your name remain.
From new moon to new moon, and from sabbath to sabbath,
all flesh shall come to worship before me, says the LORD.

Jeremiah 29:11-13
"Surely I know the plans I have for you, says the LORD,
plans for your welfare and not for harm,
to give you a future with hope.
Then when you call upon me and come and pray to me,
    I will hear you.

11. *Book of Common Worship* (Louisville: Westminster/John Knox, 1993), p. 916.

When you search for me, you will find me;
if you seek me with all your heart."

1 Peter 1:3-5
Blessed be the God and Father of our Lord Jesus Christ!
By his great mercy he has given us a new birth into a living hope
through the resurrection of Jesus Christ from the dead,
and into an inheritance that is imperishable, undefiled,
    and unfading,
kept in heaven for you, who are being protected
    by the power of God
through faith for a salvation ready to be revealed in the last time.

John 11:25-26
"I am the resurrection and the life.
Those who believe in me, even though they die, will live,
and everyone who lives and believes in me will never die."

Romans 8:38-39
For I am convinced that neither death, nor life,
nor angels, nor rulers, nor things present, nor things to come,
nor powers, nor height, nor depth, nor anything else
    in all creation,
will be able to separate us from the love of God in Christ Jesus
our Lord.

Revelation 21:3-5
"See, the home of God is among mortals.
He will dwell with them; they will be his peoples,
and God himself will be with them;
he will wipe every tear from their eyes.
Death will be no more; mourning and crying and pain
    will be no more,
for the first things have passed away."

Hymns

Below is a selection of traditional and contemporary hymns that speak in one form or another of the hope of Christ's return and/or the victory of God. A cursory review of hymnals demonstrates that this is indeed a very small sample; a great many Christian hymns have eschatological content. It might even be the case that a large percentage of churchgoers have learned their eschatology primarily from hymns.

"All Hail the Power of Jesus' Name" (Perrenot)
"O Come, O Come, Emmanuel" (Latin hymn)
"Christians All, Your Lord is Coming" (Jim Nelson, 1993)
"Jesus Shall Reign Where'er the Sun" (Watts)
"Christ the Lord Is Risen Today" (Wesley)
"Crown Him With Many Crowns" (Bridges)
"Be Still My Soul" (von Schlegel)
"Love Divine" (Wesley)
"My Hope Is Built" (Mote)
"Blessed Assurance" (Crosby)
"It Is Well with My Soul" (Spafford)
"Be Thou My Vision" (anon.)
"Lead On, O King Eternal" (Shurtleff)
"For All the Saints" (How)
"Steal Away to Jesus" (spiritual)
"Rejoice the Lord Is King" (Wesley)
"Hallelujah! What a Savior!" (Bliss)
"Lo, He Comes With Clouds Descending" (Wesley)
"Come, Thou Long Expected Jesus" (Wesley)
"The God of Abraham Praise" (David ben Judah)
"How Great Thou Art" (Boberg, Hine)
"O God, Our Help in Ages Past" (Watts)
"To God Be the Glory" (Crosby)
"Come, Christians, Join to Sing" (Bateman)

CPSIA information can be obtained at www.ICGtesting.com
Printed in the USA
BVOW03s1836091113

335839BV00003B/9/P